Heavenly Father

What about Denominations

The answer I was given after seven years serving in full time Christian ministry.

By Victor Aramanda

Acknowledgements

Thanks: Thank You Father God, for adopting me and sending Jesus to save me. Thanks to my wife for wanting to travel down this path with me. Thanks to my chaplains in the 82nd Airborne Division for being God's key disciplers when I was first born again in Saudi Arabia during the first Gulf War, especially Bart Physioc and Bob Sinnet. Thanks to my family for always loving me no matter how crazy I seemed. Thanks to the following people who God chose to use to disciple me in His ways at various times in my life: Emory and Beverly Goodman, Joshua Goodman, James and Joy Hogg, Chaplain Bart Physioc, my friends and brothers at arms in the 82nd Airborne Division's All American Chorus, Richard and Dawn Mull, Len and Robin Harper, Peter and Fiona Horrobin, Andy and Cath Taylor, the leadership of Ellel Ministries and many others that I can't list due to lack of space....

About the Author

Victor Aramanda is the younger of identical twins. He was an air-force brat who grew up in the USA, Spain, Germany, Spain, and the USA in that order, was a parachute infantryman, was in full-time ministry for more than eight years, is a husband and father, taught many conferences, lead praise and worship, lived with his family in a missionary work in the UK and in the USA, has many skills and talents.

He received the spirit of adoption from God, was born-again, on September 16, 1990 during Desert Shield while he was an infantry paratrooper in the 82nd Airborne Division. Many things happened in his life during Desert Shield, Desert Storm as well as when he returned to the United States after the first Gulf War.

Table of Contents

Why I wrote this book

This is a book written to encourage fellow Christians to find your place in the body of Christ, the church. To provide a way to think about the church so that it is seen from a point of view that may be a part of God's call for the body of Christ to come together in a new way. I hope this writing will help especially if you have encountered growing pains along the way that have stopped you from being able to join in the church as God intended. So that you can grow and be a part of His plan to help others grow too.

This book is also written to help anyone who has been called to nurture, love and teach the children of God to overcome some of the obstacles that may be hindering them from receiving the love and training which may have been being offered for years but not really being received.

"The reason I don't go to church is because they are filled with hypocrites.", is a phrase that I've heard many times spoken by people who are typically trying to keep themselves away from other people. The real reasons can be extremes, one person's could be that they don't want their own hypocrisy to be found out, while another's could be that they don't know who to trust or how to get into a community of Christians without being vulnerable, especially when someone they know has been hurt in the past by trusting.

Ultimately the excuses for not becoming a part of some group of believers, who meet on a regular basis in the name of Jesus, is about self protection in some way or another. The problem is that it is impossible to do as Jesus commands without learning to trust Him more **and** also putting yourself in a place with other believers. How else can you learn to "love one another" as He loves you. I pray that God bless you in some special way from reading what I believe He shared with me about the church.

Church

I believe the Bible teaches that the true Christian church is made up of the "people" who have been saved by God's grace through faith in His Son Jesus. People who learn, say and do what Jesus teaches them through the Holy Spirit and His Word. People who have begun, been born-again, and continue to grow in their relationship with the true and only living God according to the Christian Bible.

I believe that the church is also known as the Body of Christ, that it has many members, but is just one body. I believe that this body is spread through-out the entire world, across cultures, nations, and what are called Christians.   There is nothing wrong in something being called a "Christian" but it has become such a common term that it no longer means what was meant by its original use in the Bible in Acts chapter 11 verse 26 .

Currently the meaning of Christian may be said to be anyone, group, organization or building associated with Jesus Christ, even cults. This is dramatically different then the people of the time who lost friends, family and even life for the name. The positive side of this is that it can make it easier to be more open about saying the name of Jesus and sharing biblical truths. The negative side, which is growing more and more, is that since fewer people know what the Bible teaches, very few people know what is real and true from the Bible's point of view. I encourage anyone, really everyone reading this, to please test and investigate and consider if what I share is true. Ultimately, I hope this can help you in learning more about yourself and Jesus' call for each of us believers to be a part of His body.

I do not believe the Bible teaches that the true Christian church is an organization, any single denomination, non-denominational group, or building. I'm not against these things at all, if they allow believers to grow, are a benefit to Jesus' name being glorified and God's kingdom growing in the earth. These things can be good or bad, but the only way to know what is good or bad is to consider the point of view of the person deciding. I want to try and look at things from a Christian Biblical point of view.

If we believers in Jesus, born-again Christians, are the many members of His body "the church", then how can there be denominations? I've met pastors over the years who've been a part of church leadership groups that meet on a regular basis to share, encourage and help each other in different ways. They met for their support of one another as well as to pray and consider how God was wanting them to help in their communities even though they were not all of the same Christian denominations. I've always thought this was amazing and good, but I've also wondered how the "church", the body of Jesus here on earth, could be "one" body with many members while there seemed to be so many differences and groups.

This book is the result of an answer to an ongoing prayer I had for several years while I was in full time Christian ministry. I hope and pray that this can help you, who may be in one of three places regarding the church, get past something that could be a stumbling block in your way that I had a desire to better understand. People in three places; you, who have been born-again but have not really found or taken your place in the body of Christ, you who were in the body at some point in your life but have stepped back away from it, and you who may just be interested in a different way to consider or look at the Christian Church and denominations in this day and age we live in.

My prayer for You

Prayer

Lord Jesus, I pray for Your body, the church, to continue to come together as one in new and special ways. Please come close and help each reader to be encouraged and helped in finding the place You want them to be as a special member of Your body.

For you, the reader, I pray that Jesus would bless you, build you up, strengthen you and encourage you in many many ways. Also, I pray that He will confirm to you in your heart if you are in the place He wants you to be at this time. In Jesus's name I pray, amen.

The weigh-it, prove-it, and test-it factor

These things I share are from my heart and my beliefs, please test what I have to say. Keep what you like and leave the rest. I learned a long time ago that God is real and living, it is not my responsibility to prove that He exists to anyone, that is His responsibility. My responsibility is to share His truth in love, doing and saying what He leads me to along the way...His way.

Have you ever wondered ?

Have you ever wondered why there are different Christian groups/churches that are called denominations? Are you one of many people out there who were born-again at some point in your life but never knew where you fit in to the Christian community, the body of Christ, the church, your adopted Heavenly Father's family? Have you ever wondered how it's possible that the Bible talks about the "church ", one body of Christ Jesus when there seems to be so many? Have you ever wondered why some churches seem to say that they are the "only" community of Christian believers that will enter into heaven while the Bible does not seem to teach it that way? Have you ever had a deep desire to become part of the church without having any idea of how to do that, or why, especially when you may have seen and heard about abuses and issues with churches in the news or even by your own experience? Have you ever wondered how and when God might bring his true church together as one, some day? My prayer is that God may use what

I believe He put on my heart in some special way to shine light on some of these questions and continue the work that He is doing in you and me.

A Bugging Question

While visiting many different churches
that were part of many different Christian
denominations I had an on-going question, a
prayer really, that I believe God answered. My
question was, "Heavenly Father, why do You
allow Christian denominations to persist?
Don't they prove that there is 'not unity' and
'not oneness' in the members of the
community of believers in Jesus, the church ?
Please help me understand more clearly. ". I
served as a full-time Christian minister for more
than seven years in what are known as "para
church", non-denominational ministries. These
are ministries that come along side of churches
to help them in various ways. Many times I
went as a member of a team of ministers that
would lead praise and worship, teaching and
application of what was taught over and over,
but at different locations, and different
churches, both overseas, and in the US. I
absolutely loved being a part of something that
really helped people grow, become closer to

their Father in heaven, and really have life changing experiences.

It was amazing how the same teaching being taught over and over, but to different people, had the same end result regardless of race, nationality, location in the world, or Christian denomination. In very simple terms, with practical application, we taught the things that Jesus taught, and many truths in God's word, the Bible. By doing this we were able to be a part of Jesus's calling on our lives to help other disciples grow and even reach out to others. One of the most amazing things that I saw happen over and over was that special moment when a person is able to recognize something that they did not understand, choose to apply the new understanding, and then experience a life-changing result! Sometimes it was being able to finally forgive someone for the first time, or even more difficult for most, be able to receive and forgive themselves. Even though I was so amazed to be able to be a part of what God was continuing to do, I could not stop thinking about my on-going prayerful question, "Heavenly Father, why do You allow Christian denominations to persist, don't they prove that there is 'not unity' and 'not oneness', in the members of the community of believers in Jesus, the church ? Please help me understand them in a different way." In some ways my question came from my own past in how I became a real believer in God myself.

How I became a Christian

There was a time in my life when I realized I needed help. I knew my family and friends loved me and cared for me, but I also knew that they couldn't help me or that it was limited and partial help at best. I tried many different things to get help, but it seemed like depression and misery only grew inside and no help was ever coming.

One amazing day, as a parachute infantryman in the 82nd airborne division, during the first Gulf War, I became born again. One chaplain friend said it was as if I was just introduced to Jesus. I had followed a very simple prayer, something like, "Father God I believe that Jesus died for me to pay the price for my sins and I receive eternal life from You in Jesus's name and ask for Your forgiveness of my sins. Thank You for forgiving me. Please send Your Holy Spirit into my heart to guide me and lead me to follow after Jesus. In Jesus's name amen."   It was very simple, and at the moment that I asked for forgiveness of my sins, although it was not physical, it felt like someone had lifted a heavy backpack off of my shoulders and in its place gave me peace inside my heart and mind for the first time. That was the moment that I became born-again, and was adopted into God's family.

I now had my new Father in heaven. At that time, I asked Jesus to be Lord over everything in my life, absolutely everything. Looking back over the years I can now see that I was just a baby, and as you grow and mature, you find out that there are other things in your life that you didn't recognize when you were a baby. Things that need to be turned over to Him to take charge of and to be Lord over as you continue to grow and mature.

The more time I spent with God and applying things in life that he showed me and taught me, the more I continued to grow and grow. This included God loving and teaching me through prayer, Bible study, and fellowship with amazing Christian brothers and sisters of all levels of spiritual age and maturity. Another thing that was amazing about all of this was how these brothers and sisters, fellow real and living disciples of Jesus, came from many different Christian denominations. The "denominational name" my Christian brothers and sisters were, or had been a part of, was never an issue. The main thing always turned out to be each of our individual relationships and love for our Father in heaven, and our "love for one another as Jesus loved us".

So, what about denominations? Over the years in full-time Christian ministry I found myself praying and asking God for some understanding. Through reading and understanding, I believe that the "church", the "body of Christ", was and is "one".

However, when I looked around and saw obvious differences in organizations and "Christian" denominations I kept asking how is it possible for there to be only one true church while there is in existence multiple groupings of believers in things called denominations?

From a worldly point of view it is understandable and plain to see that denominations and churches definitely have their differences from one another. Some denominations even teach that "their membership" is the only group of "real, actual, Children of God who are going to go to heaven one day." No wonder it is so confusing, but where is God in this? What is the understanding that I believe was shared with me after many years serving many denominations, or rather, fellow brothers and sisters in Jesus? They came to our ministries for training and personal ministry themselves as well, even though they were still members of different denominations.

To begin, I believe that if God really wanted to get rid of denominations He certainly could, but it was obvious that He had not. After prayer one day, I believe that the Lord started to show me a picture. Having me look at several places throughout the New Testament where I could see something very similar to what I can see when I look at denominations. Some very important truths about people, members of denominations, non-denominational groups, and churches of the Christian faith.

In the Gospels

Throughout the gospels we see a lot of people following after Jesus. Sometimes they are called the "multitude", or "crowd". Within these, people who were also known to "gather" around or near where Jesus was, and where he was teaching and ministering, I began to see that there are several kinds of people, or ways to describe different sub-groups of people within the larger groups. Maybe it would be easier to understand these subgroups by understanding what they were doing, and why they seemed to be there listening to Jesus's teachings and staying around each other.

Let me pose it to you in the form of some questions. What were some of the different reasons that we see in the Scriptures why people wanted to be near Jesus? Some people were there because they wanted Jesus to heal them, or set them free. Some people were there because they wanted Jesus to heal someone that they knew, a friend, a family member, or even a servant for example. Some people were there because they wanted to catch Jesus doing something wrong, according to their own customs and traditions perhaps to trap or control Him, or somehow keep themselves from losing power and control over their own followers. Some people wanted to see miracles being performed, even spirits being commanded, and the amazing results for good that came in peoples' lives, real results.

Some people were actually disciples, they were not just listening but were also actually trying to apply Jesus's teachings in their lives. They would hear what he was teaching and then try to put it into practice, (that could be one of Jesus' answers to the question of "who are His disciples, even today?" which I think is seen clearly in John 8:31-32). There were times that they would hear His teaching and ask him questions to try and understand more clearly what he was saying. On more than one occasion disciples were sent out by Jesus to say and do things He told them to say and do and they had amazing testimonies, which they shared with Him upon their return. On one occasion the 12 were sent out, who are called apostles, and then another time 72 were sent out. When they returned to Jesus, they were excited and praising God about how things happened the way that Jesus said they would. One example of this is in Luke 10:17. The disciples say, "even the demons obey us when we use Your name!". He still sends out His disciples today in what is often called the "Great commission" (Mat 28:18-20, Mark 16:15-18, Lk 24:47, Jn 20:21). I can share a testimony myself of how doing the things that Jesus said and sharing and teaching the things that Jesus said still has these exciting results today. People can still be healed and set free in His name. Thank God!

Getting back to the multitudes, more specifically the subgroups within them.

Again, what were some of the reasons people were following after Jesus and being in these groups? Some were there to see signs and wonders from God, some to receive miracles and healing and freedom for themselves and others they cared for. There were also those who were "religious leaders" who were there to find out more. After closely reading through the Gospels I started to see how it was not only Jesus that was ministering and teaching, but obviously His disciples as well, just as He had told them too. One clear example of this is when Jesus returns from his transfiguration with Peter James and John, (Mat 17:14-20).

When they came down from the mountain a man shared with Jesus how Jesus' disciples we're not able to cast out an evil spirit from his son. My focus here is on the fact that the man had come to receive help for his son during the time where Jesus was up on the mountain, and the man had asked and was receiving help from Jesus' disciples who were there. What the disciples could or could not do in this instance is not my focus either, it is the fact that the disciples were doing as Jesus had been teaching them to do, ministering.

In the Early Church

After Jesus' death, burial, and resurrection moving a little forward in time we begin to see some more interesting things happening in the book of Acts in regards to groups of believers as well as their interactions with one another.

Jesus gives his disciples a command to go and wait for the gift to come from the Father, the Holy Spirit. In the upper room, behind locked doors, there were more than just 12 disciples whom the Bible says received this amazing gift. I'm not focusing here on the Holy Spirit, but the disciples.

We see the early church growing in leaps and bounds throughout the book of Acts. According to the Bible, the first time that believers were called Christians was in Antioch, (Acts 11:26).

As the apostles go throughout the land, groups of believers in Jesus begin to develop and grow. We see the Apostles continue to love and nurture these groups through letters and visits to encourage, love, and support each other towards continuing growth in following Jesus, as they were led by the Holy Spirit. Loving one another and making more disciples as Jesus commanded and guided, initially Jewish people and then Gentiles as well. The book of Acts shares how there were occasions where the apostles began to address various teachings of the time that were causing division. One example is when some groups were saying that the Gentile believers must be physically circumcised in Acts chapter 15.

Throughout the New Testament we read how the apostle Paul as well as others continue to send out teachings to groups of believers in various locations. Different groups in different locations had different areas of needs that required addressing. These teachings and letters were then sent around to other groups, in other places, and they eventually became part of the Bible, the New Testament we have today. Thank God!

So in the Gospels we see multitudes and / or crowds following Jesus that were comprised of various kinds of people for various reasons that appear to have included His own disciples, who were growing and learning from Him, as well as people that wanted to see what was going on and others who needed help for themselves and loved ones.

In the book of Acts we see the apostles, believers, disciples, and leaders of groups growing and developing in multiple countries. As we read further through the New Testament we see a variety of focuses of teaching sent out to specific localities, for example the book of Corinthian's being comprised of letters that were sent to the church, the believers in Corinth. Once again my focus is on this idea that "Christians", believers, Jesus' disciples, are all over in various countries and locations. Here in the New Testament we see how believers in different locations and cultures required focused teaching and explanation along the way. Sometimes the groups were even at odds with each other, like Jewish believers versus Gentiles. The apostles were not the only ones leading groups, or churches, there were other disciples \ believers, in these places that rose up to their callings which included loving and teaching and more. Some people caused divisions and had issues, for example, with Paul's teachings. Another obvious example is Timothy, who was mentored and encouraged by the apostle Paul on how to lead, teach and minister. Based on reading the Bible, I see that there must have been a mixture of believers and nonbelievers who heard the teachings and saw the real results of people who were continuing to grow and be Jesus' disciples. If this were not true then there would be no mention by the apostle Paul of how miracles and operating in the gifts of the Holy Spirit could impact unbelievers during times of corporate teaching, (1Co 14:22), or how we read in several places how the church continued to grow in numbers.

So just as I see the mix of people and groups of people in the multitudes and crowds following Jesus in the Gospels, I see a similar thing happening around and within the church in the book of Acts and the Epistles.

This is not a bad thing, but to be expected, even hoped for! Outside of loving your neighbor and evangelism, it is one of the ways that the church continues to grow, praise God!

What does any of this have to do with denominations?

So, What About Denominations?

For my purposes here I want to define a Christian denomination as being an established and organized group of believers following a doctrine / teaching, that has differences from other "denominations" in the practice of, and / or explanation of, and / or beliefs in some area of the Christian faith. For example, some Christian denominations "believe" that their members are the only people who will enter into heaven. Some "Believe" that God only speaks in this day and age through His written word the "Bible". Some "believe" that there is only one translation of the Bible that is true and accurate. Some believe in different days to regard as "holier" than others. Some believe that "worship" should not include the use of instruments, and the list goes on and on.

Many denominations were created when a group of believers had differences in matters of belief, to such a degree that they chose to separate and divide from each other. "Doctrinal statements" of any denomination can help to explain what some of the differences may be. I can speak from experience that I have met Christian brothers and sisters throughout my lifetime who have demonstrated loving one another the way that I believe Jesus does even though they were members of different Christian denominations. Their denominational membership had nothing to do with their love for God, his people and the world around us.

So my question to God, again, was how was it possible that there is "one" body of Christ even though there are so many "denominations"? The simple answer I believe that I received was found in looking back at what I saw in the New Testament compared to what I see demonstrated and have experienced in life and ministry across multiple denominations and non-denominational churches. I have met pastors and leaders of churches both denominational and nondenominational, who I believe to be true disciples of Jesus, with hearts to love, pastor and lead the Lord's sheep in the Lord's love. Sometimes there are definitely differences of belief and doctrine, but that does not disqualify their status of having been adopted by God. There were differences in understanding and application of God's truths in the early church between leaders, groups, and cultures just as we see happening today. Also consider what I saw in the multitudes and crowds in the Gospels, then throughout the early church regarding people's reasons for wanting to hear and see Jesus' teaching and ministry by His disciples.

So, don't be surprised if you go to any church and see a crowd, or multitude of people with similar reasons for being there like we saw in the New Testament. Apparently there is nothing new under the sun in this matter, which is no surprise.

Just because a person is a member of a church, or a member of a "denomination" does not mean that the person is a disciple of Jesus or a child of God according to the Bible. I agree with a phrase that you may have heard before from Keith Green, "going to church doesn't make you a Christian anymore then going to McDonald's makes you a hamburger." They might be there to see or hear something happen, they might be there because they need help in someway, they might be there to try to collect information against the people teaching and ministering, and yes, they may also be there as fellow brothers and sisters in the Lord who want to grow, love, and follow after the Lord's direction for them in their lives.

It is not always easy to know the difference between who is who, and I don't suppose it really matters in the big picture. What matters?

What Matters?

The "church", "the body of Christ", is one body, that is comprised of born-again children of God, saved by faith, in what Jesus did on the cross.

I don't expect the world to tell anyone the truth about God or his body, so in His love I want to be sure to share what I have learned with fellow brothers and sisters so that they too can grow without being hindered by the worldview with its lies.

You may be wondering if it is better to be a member in a denominational, or non-denominational Christian community?   My short answer is that the best place for you to be a part of, a member of, is wherever God really wants you...now. If the church is actually His body which is made up of many members, who are the people and not a building or organization, then He is the One who knows where the best place is for each member at any given time. The best any of us can do is to grow close to our Father in heaven and let Him guide us to be, and be a member of the place He wants us. It could be a group that is a part of a denomination. It could be a group that says they are non-denominational. It could be a home church, small group. It could be a group of believers meeting in a tent. I was first in a group that met when we could meet during the first Gulf War, in the Army, in Saudi Arabia. Where He wants, when He wants, for as long as He wants. That is always the best, and safest place to be in life and in fellowship with God and with our fellow brothers and sisters in His body.

In other words, I want to encourage you to run after wherever it is that the Lord leads you. A big key here is to become a part of a Christian group that meets and has fellowship on a regular basis somehow, somewhere. Spend time in prayer, in reading the Bible, and in applying whatever you learn along the way, so that you can grow in your own understanding and faith to follow Jesus and grow in your personal relationship with God.

I encourage you to seek out and find a community of Christian believers to be a part of where you can learn and grow in your faith together, where you see a demonstration of people loving each other as you see Jesus' example of that in the Bible and for you.

The Bible says that the church is the body of Christ, having many members but still one body.

Basically, if God has created you to be a big toe then pray, seek and find a community of believers where you can learn how to be a big toe. Then go and be a big toe in the body of Christ, in that group of believers. Then you will be able to experience the amazing life and plan that God has for you.

A long time ago I once heard an old evangelist say something that seemed interesting to me about denominational names. He said, "only one of two things will happen to that denominational name when you die, either it will blow off on the way up or burn off on the way down. " I don't mean to offend anyone by sharing this saying. I just want to encourage fellow brothers and sisters in the Lord to be a part of the body of Christ wherever the Lord calls you, and that if you are not in any kind of regular fellowship at this time, to find one. It is in a regular fellowship that you can be loved on by God in ways that you cannot otherwise, and that God can use you to love on and encourage other believers in some special way too.

I don't believe that God was telling me that He was going to do away with the denominations, rather that He uses them for His purpose just like everything else in time and creation, when it is all said and done. It's as if the Lord ultimately wants me to focus on His people, and loving them as He loves me, so that people inside and outside of the church, inside and outside of any denomination will see that we are His disciples.

Find Your Place in the Church

To find a fellowship, or a church, to become a part of and grow in, consider these things:

- o Do the people teach as Jesus did?
- o Do they love as Jesus loves?
- o Do they do as Jesus does?
- o Does their view and thinking of good and evil match what the Bible teaches?
- o Is their love and treatment of one another, the church, God's word, and the world demonstrating that of a caring and loving Heavenly Father?

In order to really answer these questions you will need to be reading the Bible yourself. God will keep guiding you by His Holy Spirit along the way as you keep on, keeping on. It will be worth your effort! Find a translation that you can understand and start reading today! (I currently enjoy the New International Version [NIV], and the New Living Translation [NLT], translations of the Bible.)

To keep it very simple think of it this way. The more you know what God thinks and says the easier it will be for you to compare what people, or groups of people, teach and say with what the Bible teaches and says. God will make His truth clear to you in your heart in a way that makes it understandable so that you can start knowing the direction He wants you to go with the help from His Holy Spirit.

Whenever you need to make a choice about what to do, or where to go, or what group to be a part of, His truth will come to mind and if nothing else encourage you to ask Him for His help. I don't think that anyone who teaches the Bible with a healthy fear of the Lord will have a problem if you have questions about what they teach, so ask. If you cannot receive from the person or group then maybe it is not the right place for you to be, in which case you can ask your Father in heaven for His direction in finding a group to be a part of.

He wants you to be in His body somewhere so that you can grow, and so that you can help others grow to by being who God created you to be, even as He's still working on you where you are at.

I pray that God would come and help you as you seek out His truth and way for your life, in Jesus' name, amen.

Expected Questions

Here are some questions I expect to hear from my brothers and sisters….

- How do I find a group of believers to become a part of?
  - Pray, "Father God, please help me find a Christian group to be a part of so that I can be in the place in Your body where you want me to be. In Jesus' name I pray, amen."
- Is it wrong to be a member of a denomination?
  - No, unless you are convicted by the Lord otherwise, and / or it becomes clear that doing so is spiritually unhealthy or their doctrine is in error.

- Is it wrong to be excited of what my denomination or group is doing?
  - No, just keep asking if you are where God wants you to be.
- Is it better to be a member of a non-denominational church?
  - No, unless you are convicted by the Lord otherwise, and / or it becomes clear that doing so is spiritually unhealthy or their doctrine is in error.
- What can I do if I love the group I'm a member of but there seems to be teaching that does not seem to be Biblically true?
  - Do what the Bible teaches in Mat 18:15-17, and in Titus 3:10-11. Ultimately this can be hard but healthy. I'd recommend to read

these verses with someone you trust in the Lord and His word and prayerfully consider how the Lord leads you. It could mean the teaching changes, or that the person teaching leaves, or that you are led somewhere else yourself.

- When I look for a church or group to become a part of, how do I know if they are teaching what the Bible does or not?
    - You must be studying and reading and learning what the Bible teaches yourself so you can compare what the Bible teaches to what you are hearing.
    - The Holy Spirit will help guide you in truth
    - God's love should be present and the love for the sheep of God.

○ One pastor I knew and respected use to say, "Beware of a shepherd who does not smell of sheep."

My Hope for You

Christian Brothers and Sisters

So many groups and churches call themselves Christian and it can be confusing to know where to go, or what group to be a part of so that you can grow in your own faith. Ultimately my prayer and hope is to encourage and help you to take a step of faith and find your place in the body of Christ, the church. Especially all of you who have not known where to go, or how to recognize a group to become a part of, so you can help others grow, as well as grow more yourselves too.

Don't let Denominations keep you away from taking your place in the body of Christ

To keep it simple I want to say that denominations come in many sizes. So do churches, both denominational and non-denominational. If there is an obvious pro to any really large group it is that these large groups can do a lot! In communities and in the world. Think of the apostle Paul, he did not shy away from being a Roman citizen, but used that part of who he was meant to be for God. That citizenship was used by God through Paul to help in continuing to grow the church! Large groups and membership in them are also used by God, so are the small! If you want to know whether or not a group is of who we Christians believe is God then you'd have to compare teaching and character and love of people with what the Bible teaches the same as I encourage you to do with any other group. I'm not against any large group or organization, but I challenge everyone to consider if they are where the Lord wants them to be. If they are then fantastic. If not, then ask and pray what you are to do for yourself, your family, and the church. It could be to go, stay, be a part of change, be a silent and prayerful example….

Maybe another way to consider things would be to answer this question of any group no matter the size. Whose disciples are they making? Am I where the Lord wants me. My simple prayer goes something like this.

"Heavenly Father, I want to be wherever You want me, for as long as You want me there, with whoever You want me there with. Please guide and lead me by Your Holy Spirit I pray, in Jesus' name. Amen."

My Hope for Church Leaders

I encourage you church leaders to run after the Lord's call on your life. I have met church leaders that love God and His children in a manner that was obviously from God. They were not always in agreement with the doctrine of their denomination, but were able to dis-agree agreeably and stay in the denomination. There are some who find that they are called out from their denomination or into new ministries, or even to go and be a part of some other existing one. I want to encourage you that you are not alone in following the Lord Jesus, so cry out if you need help and ask Him to make His way for you clear so you can run after it.

A Thought about Hypocrisy

What about the hypocrisy in the church? I think this has a lot to do with your point of view and understanding of people.

Often I think that it'd be wise to consider that who we may call hypocrite could be a person who is like the rest of us. Growing and human. Just because we know what we ought to do, does not always mean we are able. There are times when immaturity and a lack of understanding are the real issue.

What if the person needs to grow or maybe even needs to have someone come alongside and in love, help and encourage them. Perhaps even rebuke, but all in love. There are some people who are practicing hypocrisy, but probably not as many as there are spiritually young Christians who need help in growing. Maybe you are a part of God's help.

Last Thoughts

Perhaps I could write more about how to compare church doctrines with each other and the Bible. Or maybe how to find out if a group has occult practices and teaching. Another interesting topic could be about the 5-fold ministry mentioned in Ephesians 4:11. Ultimately the Lord Jesus says that He will guide His sheep by His Holy Spirit. So I want to end by encouraging many to begin. Begin speaking to God out loud in prayer, ask Him to help you know His truth and to be able to get closer to Him by finding your place in regular Christian fellowship, the body of Christ Jesus, the church.

Father, I pray that churches will be able to continue to work with each other more and more putting aside their differences when possible to raise up Jesus' disciple in His ways. I also pray that You would raise up, encourage and strengthen Your apostles, prophets, evangelists, pastors, and teachers to help the church in our day continue to grow, in Jesus' name.

The simple key in the end is to focus on Jesus' teachings through the Bible and apply them in your life as you can. Find people who seem to know God and His word, the Bible, who love as you see Jesus love, and begin to spend time with them. Don't let the fact that a church is, or is not, a part of a denomination scare you away from where God calls you to go and become a part of so you can grow and help others grow too.

Some encouraging Bible verses.

So you have not received the spirit that makes you fearful slaves. Instead, you received God's Spirit when he adopted you as his own children. Now we call him, "Abba, Father." For his spirit joins with our spirit to affirm that we are God's children. (Romans 8:15–16 NLT)

Whoever does God's will is my brother and sister and mother. (Mark 3:35 NIV)

To the Jews who had believed him, Jesus said, "If you hold to my teaching, you are really my disciples. (John 8:31 NIV)

Now this is eternal life: that they know you, the only true God, and Jesus Christ, whom you have sent. (John 17:3 NIV)

Recommended Resources

Bible Translations:

New Living Translation, (NLT)

New International Version, (NIV)

The Amplified Bible

Holman Christian Standard Bible, (HCSB)

English Standard Version, (ESV)

Personal growth:

God's Adopted

By Victor D. Aramanda

The Jesus Training Manual

By Richard Mull

The Most Powerful Prayer On Earth

By Peter Horrobin